A Quiz about the
Man in Your Life

Do You Know Your Groom?

DAN CARLINS

$\mathcal{Y}$ou may think you know almost everything there is to know about the man you've chosen as your groom. Trust us, this little book will show that really, you don't.

No matter how long you two have known each other, no matter how much you've talked—about matters both serious and foolish—there's plenty you haven't yet learned about him.

This hundred-question quiz will help you to educate yourself, so grab a pencil and see how you do. You won't find the answers in the book, of course. For those, you'll have to check with your groom. When you do, you'll find yourselves talking to each other about each other: your likes and dislikes, your beliefs and opinions, and stories and facts about your pasts.

They're little things, sure, but they aren't insignificant. They're the bits and pieces that make up who we are. And knowing about them is much more than collecting mere personal trivia. Knowing is caring.

Score ten points for each correct answer (taking partial credit wherever you can) and rate yourself according to this scale:

> **Above 900:** What a performance!
>
> **800–900:** Very good for a couple just starting out.
>
> **600–790:** Pretty good. You'll improve as time goes by.
>
> **Below 600:** Ask your groom for a remedial course.

Good luck.

—D.C.

1. **Does your groom know his own car license plate number?**

    ____ Yes

    ____ Almost

    ____ Not even close

2. **What nicknames has he gone by, from childhood on?**

3. **Does he think a guy who gets regular manicures is:**

    ____ Properly concerned about the health and appearance
    of his nails?

    ____ Too vain?

    ____ Too lazy to clip his own nails?

4. **Has he ever taken lessons on a musical instrument?**

    ____ Yes, he's studied the _____.

    ____ No

5. **Does your groom think eating dinner in bed is:**

    ____ Great—he'd do it every day if he could?

    ____ OK on rare occasions?

    ____ Too messy to even contemplate?

6. **Would he rather:**

   _____ Play a board game?

   _____ Go dancing?

   _____ Explore a city he's never been to?

   _____ Bike ride in the country?

7. **If he won a huge lottery prize, what's the first thing he'd do?**

   _____ Party   _____ Look for a new house

   _____ Quit his job   _____ Find a financial adviser

8. **If he finds himself at a really bad movie, would he rather:**

   _____ Leave?

   _____ Sit it out and complain later?

9. **If served raw oysters, will he:**

   _____ Devour them?   _____ Turn them down?

   _____ Pick at them?   _____ Hide them?

10. **Is there a favorite family recipe that your groom thinks should be preserved for posterity?**

    _____ Yes, his _____'s recipe for

    _____.

    _____ No

11. Has he ever kicked a bad habit?

____ Yes, he stopped _____.

____ No, he never has.

12. Does he have any habits now that he'd like to beat?

____ Yes, he wants to quit _____.

____ No, he doesn't.

13. Does your groom consider a walk on the beach in winter:

____ Romantic?   ____ A waste of time?

14. Can he type without looking at the keyboard?

____Very well   ____ Not at all

____ OK

15. Can he use a remote without looking at the buttons?

____ Easily   ____ No

____ If he feels around a bit

16. Does he know the birthdays of at least six people other than his immediate family?

____ Yes, at least that many.

____ No, but he does know a few.

____ He barely knows his own.

17. When was the last time he stayed up all night?

____ Less than a week ago   ____ It's been ages

____ Less than a year ago   ____ Probably never

18. Does he now know, or has he ever personally known:

____ A circus performer?   ____ A mobster?

____ An orchestra conductor?   ____ A TV weathercaster?

19. What junk food can't he stay away from?

20. Most days, would he rather:

____ Go to a party?

____ Hang out with a couple of friends?

____ Be by himself?

21. Does he think giving kids a firm bedtime is:

____ A must for a peaceful household?

____ Impossible to enforce, so forget it?

____ Unnecessary, since they'll go to sleep when they're tired?

22. If you asked him, would your groom spend a Saturday morning going to yard sales or church rummage sales?

____ Happily   ____ Unenthusiastically

____ Only if dragged   ____ Only if drugged

23. Which category or categories would he use to describe himself in high school?

____ Prep   ____ Partygoer

____ Nerd   ____ Goth

____ Gang member   ____ Jock

____ Outsider   ____ Freak

____ Middle-of-the-roader   ____ Sports fan

24. Someone cuts in front of the two of you in a movie line. Will your groom:

____ Tell the intruder to get back where he belongs?

____ Mutter quietly to you but say nothing?

____ Pretend not to notice?

25. A friend borrows $20 and forgets to pay it back. Will he:

____ Remind the friend?

____ Drop a hint?

____ Keep silent to avoid embarrassing the friend?

____ Forget about it himself?

26. If asked to name his all-time favorite movie, he'll say:

____ "It's _____."

____ "I can't choose just one."

____ "I'm not a big moviegoer."

27. He believes that dreams can predict the future.

____ Yes   ____ No way

____ Sometimes

28. Would he be a contestant on a big-money TV game show?

____ He'd do it in a flash.   ____ You've got to be kidding!

____ If you urged him to.

29. Of the people from his past he's in touch with, other than family, which one has he known the longest?

30. Does your groom know what color your eyes are?

____ Yes   ____ No way

____ No, but he'll try to guess

31. What's his mother's maiden name?

32. Does he know your mother's maiden name?

_____ Yes   _____ No

33. If you ask him to recite "Mary Had a Little Lamb," how will he do?

_____ He'll recite it easily.

_____ He'll stumble, but more or less get it right.

_____ He'll mess up.

34. Of all the teachers he ever had, which one does he consider the hottest?

35. What does he think of watching television during mealtime?

_____ It's OK if others want to watch too.

_____ It's OK anytime—let others talk among themselves if they don't want to watch.

_____ It's rude, distracting, and unacceptable.

36. To start the morning, does your groom:

____ Always want a big breakfast?

____ Want at least a little something to eat?

____ Happily start the day on an empty stomach?

37. Is he comfortable eating a full meal in a restaurant alone?

____ He'll dine alone anytime.

____ He'll eat solo if necessary, but he'd prefer not to.

____ He'd rather grab a candy bar from a vending machine.

38. In the bank, after the teller counts out his money, does he re-count it? Does he double-check money from an ATM or accept the machine's count? How about change from a store clerk?

	COUNTS	DOESN'T COUNT
TELLER		
ATM		
CLERK		

39. Does he generally aim to arrive at appointments:

____ Ahead of time?

____ Just on time?

____ No more than a few minutes late?

____ Whenever he gets there?

40. Does your groom:

_____ Slide his chair back under the table when he gets up?

_____ Close drawers, cupboard doors, and closet doors when he's done with them?

_____ Choose the piece of fruit that's getting dangerously close to overripe?

41. "What happened to the guy who ran right through the screen door?" "He strained himself." Your groom will judge this joke:

_____ Worth a big laugh.

_____ OK.

_____ Much too, er, strained.

42. Appliance manuals and warranty cards—Does he:

_____ Keep them?   _____ Pitch them?

43. "Never do business with a friend."

_____ He agrees.   _____ He disagrees.

44. Which of these make him very uncomfortable?

_____ Small, enclosed spaces   _____ Crowded areas

_____ Being completely alone   _____ Deep water

_____ Large, out-of-control dogs   _____ The thought of growing old

45. He has nightmares:

____ Often   ____ Rarely

____ Occasionally   ____ Never

46. Are his eyes equal in strength or is one stronger?

____ They're equal.

____ The _____ eye is stronger.

47. When told about a married couple with separate bedrooms, your groom thinks:

____ If it works for them, fine.

____ There's probably something wrong.

____ Who knows what goes on in other people's lives?

48. He's invited to a dinner party and offered a chance to choose his table partner, knowing nothing but the occupation of each guest. Which of these would your groom pick to sit next to?

____ Newspaper reporter   ____ Librarian

____ Minister   ____ Fish distributor

____ Firefighter   ____ Teacher

49. Can he:

____ Jump rope?   ____ Play jacks?

____ Spin a Hula-hoop?   ____ Juggle?

50. Which type of vehicle has he ever driven—even once?

____ Convertible   ____ Pickup

____ Bus   ____ Large truck

____ Motorcycle   ____ Boat

51. How did his parents meet?

52. Would he rather take vacations to:

____ The same place over and over, for familiarity and comfort?

____ Different places each time, for variety and adventure?

____ Some of both?

53. How many of Snow White's Seven Dwarfs can he name?

____ None

____ One to three

____ Four to six

____ All seven (Happy, Grumpy, Dopey,
Sleepy, Sneezy, Bashful, and Doc)

54. When was he last inside a hospital, either as a patient or visitor? Explain.

55. Does your groom think couples should have a night out without each other:

____ Often   ____ Never

____ Occasionally

56. At the beach, does he prefer:

____ Lying in the sun?   ____ Playing in or walking on the sand?

____ Walking on the rocks?

____ Lying under an umbrella?   ____ None of the above?

57. As a child, did he ever go to summer camp? (Ten bonus points if you can name the camp—unless you went there too.)

____ Yes, he went to _____.

____ No, he wasn't a camper.

58. Where were his parents born?

Mother: _____

Father: _____

59. If he thought a mechanic had cheated him, would he:

_____ Keep quiet and pay?

_____ Point out the problem and ask that it be fixed?

_____ Loudly refuse to pay and make a fuss?

60. The last time he was in a fistfight was:

_____ This month   _____ In the past five years

_____ This year   _____ A long time ago, if ever

61. What's his most memorable childhood vacation?

62. Does he try to answer the phone on the first, second, or third ring, or does he not count?

_____ First   _____ Third

_____ Second   _____ Whichever

63. Has he ever been unconscious? Why?

_____ Yes, because _____.

_____ He hasn't.

64. Has he ever:

____ Bungee jumped?

____ Ridden an animal other than a horse?

____ Been a pallbearer?

____ Twirled pizza dough in the air?

65. Which sport has he never played, even once?

____ Soccer

____ Lacrosse

____ Golf

____ Softball

____ Rugby

____ He's played all of these

66. What does he think is the funniest comedy series ever?

67. "A meal without dessert isn't really a meal." Your groom would:

____ Agree

____ Disagree

68. Within two, how many keys does he usually carry?

69. Does he know how many rings his mother wears?

____ Yes

____ No

70. Does he enjoy:

_____ Walking barefoot?   _____ Listening to music?

_____ Watching a rodeo?   _____ Climbing trees?

71. Has he ever known anyone with one of these nicknames?

_____ Tiny   _____ Peanut

_____ Baldy   _____ Pinky

_____ Red   _____ Moose

72. Has his name ever appeared in a news headline?

_____ Yes, because _____.

_____ No, but it's been in an article.

_____ No, but he's written a letter to the editor that's been published.

_____ No, never.

73. Has he ever had a boss he truly liked and respected? Who?

_____ Yes: _____

_____ Never

74. Does he consider himself:

_____ A good joke teller?

_____ Not much of a joke teller but a good critic?

_____ Not really a joke person?

75. Which of these can he locate?

____ The Parthenon   ____ Pamplona

____ Mont Saint Michel   ____ Machu Picchu

____ Monticello   ____ None of 'em

76. Does your groom think dogs and cats:

____ Should never be fed table scraps?

____ Can be fed from the table, at least occasionally?

77. In hot weather, which does he prefer?

____ Air conditioning

____ Fans

____ Toughing it out

78. During the past year, has he considered growing a beard or mustache? If he has one, has he considered shaving it?

____ He's toyed with the idea.

____ The thought hasn't crossed his mind.

79. During the past year, has he considered getting a tattoo? If he has one, has he considered having it removed?

____ He's toyed with the idea.

____ The thought hasn't crossed his mind.

80. Two years before you decided to marry, would he have guessed that he'd be getting engaged within that time period? How about one year before?

	2 YEARS	1 YEAR
ABSOLUTELY		
MAYBE		
NO WAY		

81. Does he remember much about your first date together?

____ Yes, in great detail.

____ He remembers a little about it.

____ The event is gone from his memory.

82. Is there any household chore that your groom actually enjoys?

____ Yes: _____

____ None whatsoever

83. When asked as a child what HE wanted to be when he grew up, he answered:

84. Where does he usually carry his wallet?
(Ten bonus points if you know what color his wallet is.)

85. Fooling around in an office, has he ever photocopied a part of his body?

_____ Glad to say he hasn't.   _____ Sorry, he has.

86. Does he have a boyhood friend who has become:

_____ A clergyman?   _____ A grade school teacher?

_____ A rock musician?   _____ A policeman?

_____ A railroad conductor?   _____ A doctor?

87. What's he better at?

_____ Darts   or   _____ Ping-Pong

_____ Omelets   or   _____ Scrambled eggs

_____ Hearing   or   _____ Smelling

88. Does your groom have a scar anywhere other than on his face or arms?

_____ Yes, on his _____.

_____ Not a one.

89. If he had a twelve-year-old daughter who needed her vision corrected and could have either eyeglasses or contacts, which would he urge her to wear? What about a son?

	DAUGHTER	SON
EYEGLASSES		
CONTACTS		

90. Does he know Pig Latin?

____ Esyay   ____ Onay

91. Has he ever binge-watched:

____ For more than four episodes of any series in one sitting?

____ For more than six episodes?

____ For more than eight?

92. Does he think he looks his best:

____ In casual clothes?   ____ In nothing at all?

____ Dressed up?   ____ In anything?

93. Does he have any former friends he now intentionally avoids? Who?

____ Yes: _____

____ No

94. Does your groom have anything that was once owned by one of his grandparents? By one of his great-grandparents?

____ Yes, a grandparent's: _____

____ Yes, a great-grandparent's: _____

____ Nothing

95. How well does he remember phone numbers? Does he know:

____ His family's number from his childhood?

____ Any number he had in school?

____ The first number he had of his own?

____ The number at his first full-time job?

96. Does he know who Charlie Parker was?

____ Sure: the bebop-era alto sax player.

____ No, he knows very little about jazz.

97. Which relative or good friend drives him the craziest?

98. How many articles of clothing does he have that are more than six years old?

____ None

____ At least one

____ Several

____ Pretty much his whole wardrobe

99. How many vegetarians does he know?

____ None or one

____ Two to five

____ More than five

100. "The best restaurant meal in the world isn't as enjoyable as a good meal at home." Would he:

____ Agree?

____ Disagree?

____ Say "Well, that depends…"?

This publication is designed to provide accurate and authoritative information in regard to the
subject matter covered. It is sold with the understanding that the publisher is not engaged
in rendering legal, accounting, or other professional service. If legal advice or other expert
assistance is required, the services of a competent professional person should be sought.
—From a Declaration of Principles Jointly Adopted by a Committee of the American Bar
Association and a Committee of Publishers and Associations

All brand names and product names used in this book are trademarks, registered
trademarks, or trade names of their respective holders. Sourcebooks is not associated with
any product or vendor in this book.

Published by Sourcebooks
P.O. Box 4410, Naperville, Illinois 60567–4410
(630) 961-3900
sourcebooks.com

Library of Congress Cataloging-in-Publication data is on file with the publisher

Printed and bound in the United States of America.

DR 10 9 8 7 6 5 4 3 2 1